Also by Frank West:
From Guilt to the Gift of Miracles
Healing Our Anger
Healing Our Special Relationships

A CASE OF MISTAKEN IDENTITY

by

Frank West

ISBN: 1466392401
ISBN-13: 978-1466392403

I dedicate this work to my beloved late wife Martha who taught me the meaning of Love. She has been and still remains my collaborator, inspiration and guide, patiently and gently leading me toward a clearer vision of the Truth.

CONTENTS

PREFACE

This little volume is the last in a series of three that deal with key ideas found in the spiritual/psychological writings scribed by Dr. Helen Schucman more than a generation ago and known as *A Course in Miracles*. It consists of material from two workshops I presented in 2011 on the subject of our mistaken identity; that is, our tendency to see ourselves not as the holy Sons and Daughters of God—which is our true identity—but, rather, as "the home of evil, darkness and sin," the mistaken identity of the ego. Our work consists in healing this erroneous perception so that we begin to identify ourselves, correctly, as the spirit of Love. The first talk occurred February 23 at Drew University in Madison, New Jersey; the second on July 16 at the First Unitarian Church of Portland, Maine.

The ideas as I treat them here are grounded in my own personal experiences of a lifetime that (so far) has lasted over eighty-five years.

Frank West
Guilford, Connecticut
Summer 2011

ACKNOWLEDGEMENT

I'm grateful for the thoughtful editing of this work by my friend Chad Hardin, musician, composer and master of the written word. Without his efforts—or his sure feel for the tone and cadence of my particular voice—this book could not have come to be.

1
BEGINNING

Some of you, I know, are in groups that study *A Course in Miracles*, while some of you may not have had any experience with the spiritual path called by (strange name!) *A Course in Miracles*. How many here don't know anything about the Course? (*Counting the raised hands*) One, two—three of you. Okay, then, I'm going to spend some time just talking about how the Course came to be, and something about the ideas it proposes.

I'd like you to know that my main interest in presenting this workshop is not only to impart what I've learned. The Course has given me a peace of mind, and I want to share what's been good for me with you. That, by the way, is the purpose of our lives as the Course sees it, that we heal our minds so that we can reflect the love of God to our brothers. And that brings us deep happiness. There *is* no other happiness but that. That's why I'm happy to be here doing what I'm about to do. And I hope you will find that happiness too.

I'm mostly interested in the question and answer periods, the discussion periods. I've written three books and people tell me, "The best part of your books, Frank, are when people ask questions and there's a discussion." So please, I beg of you, ask questions. There's going to be five periods in which you can ask questions.

The five stages of my talk will be, first, an introduction about what the Course is and how it came to be. Then there will a question and answer period, and I'd like to hear then from group members what their experience has been studying the Course. Secondly, I'd like to describe the metaphysical basis of the Course's philosophy. Every spiritual path has it's "mythology." And the Course has its own mythology. It's true that myths are not in themselves real, but they do help us understand why we are acting as strangely as we act; and why we have the peace we have when we have it.

The third part of the talk will be a description of our mind. The Course's view is that we have a seemingly split mind—split into three parts. And I will illustrate that split with a diagram I've drawn over here on the board in preparation for this talk (after I've unveiled it!).

The fourth section of the talk will be a description of the so-called ego; that is, the part of our mind that is hurtful to us. It's bodily-based; and it's a totally false self. That's why the subtitle for this talk is "A Case of Mistaken Identity." We identify—mistakenly—with our bodies, and then all hell breaks loose. And I will describe exactly why it *is* hell when we identify ourselves with our bodies.

Then we'll have a break, after—again—some discussion of what I've laid out. And then, in the final section of the talk, I'll describe the spiritual part of our mind, which is what the Course calls the Holy Spirit; the Holy Spirit *in* our mind. It also refers to it as the Right Mind; in fact, it's the *only* mind—since the ego basically is unreal, has never been, is a myth that we *think* is real—the only reality being Love.

That's the Course's idea: the only reality is Love. And everything else—including everything you see in this room—is not real. Now that's a very hard thing to get. There's a line in the Course: "There is no world." To which most of us would respond, "No world!? You gotta be kidding!"

Well, I'll tell you a story that illustrates this difficult concept, that there is no world. I know a woman who, on the island of Mykonos, went to a concert. She was sitting in the last row, with no one behind her. And during that concert, on four occasions, the upper part of her body was pushed forward, forcibly, by some unseen force behind her. This startled and amazed her of course.

Well, I happened to be telling her story to my oldest daughter. My oldest daughter is, I think, an advanced soul. I have a notion that she and I have been around—along with her mom—for a number of lifetimes, in various forms. My daughter is an interdenominational minister out on the West coast. She's very spiritual: started out in Hinduism, went on to Buddhism, and now is into the Course and runs a Course study group.

So I'm telling her the story of the woman on Mykonos and she says, "Dad, I had a similar experience at age eight. I was afraid to tell you about the experience then, because I thought you would have me institutionalized." And I said, "Well, tell me what the experience was and I'll tell you whether I would have had you institutionalized or not!"

So she said, "Dad, remember when we lived at 100th Street and Riverside Drive in Manhattan?" And I said, "Oh yeah." (We'd moved to Manhattan, from a three-church rural parish in Ohio where I was minister, so that I could study psychoanalysis. I was supporting a wife and three children, with a fourth on the way, on a $5000 annual grant—I can tell you we ate a lot of beans in those days!)

Anyway, my daughter said, "You remember I attended P.S. 75 at the corner of 96th and Riverside?" I said, "Yeah." "Well, my routine when school let out," she said, "would be to walk up West End Avenue to 100th Street and then walk over to our apartment." "I remember that," I said. She said, "Dad, somewhere around age eight, I was walking home from school, when suddenly I was pushed into the building at the southwest corner of West End Avenue and 100th Street by a powerful and invisible force. And I heard a voice saying to me, *Laura, look around. Everything you see is a movie that you have made up.*

I said to her, "Had you come home and told me that then, I sure would have had you institutionalized! Or at the very least called a psychiatrist. But now, I embrace you—because you heard the truth."

What we see "out there," folks, is a projection from our mind, and is not a part of reality. The only reality is the Love in our hearts; a

Love that we all share. That's the Course's idea. You might have some trouble with that. Many do. I have had trouble with that in the past. I don't now.

So finally, after we have a discussion of that spiritual part, we will have a brief meditation; and then we'll be at the end of the day.

2

WHAT THE COURSE IS AND HOW IT CAME TO BE

So let me start. For those of you who have had no understanding of *A Course in Miracles*, it is non-dualistic, which means it does not believe in an "evil power." It *does* say that a lot of evil things happen in the world; but *we* do it, and we do it as the result of a mistaken choice on our part, not because of some evil power. Since only Love is real, therefore, the Course is not dualistic.

The Course is also psychologically sophisticated. The psychology in the Course basically couldn't have been written without Freud; meaning that its psychology is neo-Freudian, resembling in many ways the so-called British school of psychoanalysis: Michael Balint, D.W. Winnicott, Anna Freud and others, all whose work I studied when I came to Manhattan in the 1950s. Therefore when I encountered the Course some decades afterwards, I really got into it, because the psychology was just what I'd understood, especially the Course's understanding of *projection* of our feelings and thoughts out onto others; especially dumping our guilt and our hate onto somebody else (which I'll talk about a little later).

The third thing about the Course is that its spiritual path is based on the study of interpersonal relationships. And since we're always bumping into people, all the time, we have plenty of opportunity for what we might call a meditative experience in studying what our reactions are to the various people who cross our path. I like that idea, because it means that the peace that I gain by healing my mind through studying my interactions with other people makes possible a more peaceful exchange with others. And then others are drawn to me. In fact, I believe you too will experience this as you heal your minds—people being drawn to you saying, "I want what you have."

Let me illustrate. I have a patient who was very happy with what I'd done for her, so when she finished her work with me, she said, "Frank, I'd like to take you out to lunch, to celebrate our relationship." I said, "Oh, that's cool. I like going to lunch." And she said, "I'll pick up the tab," and I said, "Oh good, that's even better." So she picks me up and takes me to lunch. And after lunch, I say to her, "Let's stop by this new art gallery in town. They really have some great stuff there—Madison Avenue quality."

So we stop at this gallery, and when we go in, my patient meets a woman she knows, a fellow teacher, and they begin chatting, while I stand there. And then this woman looks at me for the first time, and her eyes bug out. And she says to me, "Could I stand near you?" And I said, "Sure." So she came up and stood near me. Her husband was there, and her daughter who'd just graduated from Skidmore. And this woman said, "Could I possibly hug you?" And I said, "Sure, I'll give you a hug." So I gave her a hug. It took a long time for her to part from me. And she said, "I don't know what there is about you, but I just want to be near you." And her daughter said, "Can I have a hug too?" And I said, "Sure!" So I gave the daughter a hug. Of course the husband hung back. Men usually hang back. So I say to the husband, "Why don't you join us?" So all three of them are now hugging me!

Well, all of this time, my patient—who's very volatile—was saying, "Oh, my God. Oh, my God. Oh, my God!" So what I understood from that situation was that—to the extent that I have healed my mind from the egotism, the hate, the *murderous* hate that was in my heart for so long—I now was in a different state, and there was an attraction there.

Let me read you a quote from the Course that addresses just this phenomenon:

"There is a light that this world cannot give. Yet you can give it, as it was given you. And as you give it, it shines forth to call you from the world and follow it. For this light will attract you as nothing in the world can do. You will lay aside this world and find another. And here will everything remind you of your Father and His holy Son. And your light will attract others who will shine on you as you shine on them. In their gratitude they will shine on you because you brought them here. Your light will join with theirs in a power so compelling that it will draw others out of darkness to look on them." (T-13.VI.11)[1]

That's what can happen, I believe, as you study and give up your egotism. There is a wonderful connection that you will establish, in the strangest ways, that are just unexpected. And that's why they're miraculous.

The Course stresses that everything happens in the mind. It's not interested in behavior. It doesn't care what you do. It does care about the motivation for *why* you're doing it. So it doesn't focus at all on behavior; it focuses on your mind. And if you choose to be in what the Course calls the Right Mind—which I will illustrate a little later on with my diagram—then you will have an ethical, kind and generous attitude toward the world. You won't have to worry about the ethics—the appropriate behavior will follow the right-minded choice.

It's also true that the Course aims at ending the idea of sacrifice. "Shoulds" and "oughts," "responsibilities," "duties" are not words that apply to the Right Mind—they are egotistical concepts based on guilt. Because God only wants your happiness! He doesn't care about the "shoulds" and the "oughts" of life, which often lead to our sacrificing. Now that also means the Course deviates from mainstream Christian ideas, because Christianity is based on the idea of sacrifice: the sacrifice of Jesus which somehow magically heals our minds. I could never really believe that. So I was glad to find a spiritual path that said that sacrifice is an ego-thought, and has no part in Love. Rather, sacrifice has to do with Loss. Someone loses.

---

1 This is the standard annotation referencing *A Course in Miracles*. The Course consists of a text, a workbook, and a manual for teachers. In the annotation above, *T* stands for text, *13* is the chapter number, *VI* is the section within the chapter, and *11* is the paragraph number of that section.

Finally the Course posits that the experience of healing the mind is a gradual process in which little steps are taken to make corrections. Basically it means changing our identification from our body to identification with spirit; spirit being Love. It focuses on removing the egotism—the fear, guilt and hate—by forgiveness. And it requires vigilance and diligence and a capacity to look within, and to admit that you've been wrong in your ideas. And its main purpose is to urge you always to ask, "What is the *purpose* for any of my behaviors, or any of my thoughts?"

Those are a few of the ideas that I believe the Course is all about. Now let me read you how it came to be, for those of you who have not yet had the experience of knowing the Course. I'm going to read from the introduction to *From Guilt to the Gift of Miracles*, which is one of my books.

"A Course in Miracles *began when Helen Schucman and William Thetford, both professors of medical psychology at Columbia University's College of Physicians and Surgeons, in New York, decided to join in a common goal. In the words of Helen (who was a specialist in working with psychotics at Columbia):*

Psychologist, educator, conservative in theory, and atheistic in belief..."

Very interesting—*atheistic* in belief!

"...I was working in a prestigious and highly academic setting; and then something happened that triggered a chain of events I could never have predicted. The head of my department unexpectedly announced that he was tired of the angry and aggressive feelings our attitudes reflected, and concluded that 'there must be a better way.' As if on cue, I agreed to help him find it. Apparently this Course is the 'other way.'

To paraphrase what happened next: for three startling months preceding the actual writing, Bill had suggested that Helen write down the highly symbolic dreams and descriptions of the strange images she was experiencing. Although she had become fairly accustomed to the unexpected by that time, she was still surprised the day that she wrote: 'This is a course in miracles—' her introduction to a Voice. Though she heard no outer sound, Helen began to receive a kind of rapid inner dictation, which she wrote down and saved in a shorthand notebook. The writing was never automatic, for she could be interrupted at any time and later instantly listen to the Voice again at will."

(In other words, Helen could be in the middle of writing down a sentence, be interrupted by a telephone call; and when the call was over, the sentence would continue as if there had been no interruption.)

"Though it felt strange and very uncomfortable, Helen never seriously felt any need to stop it, as if it were a special assignment that she had somewhere, somehow agreed to complete. The long collaborative venture that ensued between Bill and Helen became a strong and significant part of the whole project."

An interesting thing is that Helen never really "got it." She got the Course *intellectually*; but she was never able to live it. And I think that's even more compelling evidence—to me—that this Course is true. Because if Helen had gotten it, we could say, "Well, those are just *her* ideas." (By the way, I hope that she gets it "the next time around." I'm sure that she will! And that's because the Course posits that *we all get it*, eventually. The outcome is certain. *Certain*. We *will* go home and have the peace that we deserve to have.)

⌘   ⌘   ⌘

Okay, let me ask those of you in the audience here: Can you share your experience of what the Course has meant to you? Or do you have any questions about what I just said? Or additions to what I may not have said—since I don't know it all?

Q. I was thinking about this just today—and of course, I have different thoughts at different times—but the Course has really brought me a sense of freedom. Moments of freedom. I knew what freedom felt like, but the Course has liberated my entire life; so that

I'm free to choose almost all the time. Freedom to play, and have a good time. I know now that everything's okay. I have a sense of—of contentment, I guess you could call it. I've been working with the Course since 1982.

A. Good for you. Thank you very much for that. It's an affirmation. Anybody else? By the way, please speak up when you ask your questions. I have only half an ear, you see. I left the other half in Germany in World War II. So forgive me if I have to listen hard.

Q. I was raised Catholic. I went to Catholic schools as a child. Yet I'm always looking around for other churches. Today I go to the Catholic church, but also I go to the Assembly of God church. And when you said there is no evil, I question that; because I do believe there is a Satan. But if I do not recognize him, he doesn't exist. And I think always I've been searching and looking for and feeling him. So I think part of the problem is I have to get the ego out of the way, and question why I do things. I always try to do what I think other people would do. But at the same time I pat myself on the back, like the Pharisees.

I can very easily understand and identify with your Course. You mentioned how people spontaneously want to hug you; how they recognize the goodness in you. Well, there were some missionaries that came to my church; and they were talking about when they were recently in Bucharest, which is in one of these atheistic countries in Eastern Europe. And this woman came up to them and said, "May I ask you a personal question?" And they said, "Certainly." So she asked, "Are you Christians?" And they said, "Yes." And she said, "I've heard of Christians, but I've never actually seen one before." So I can identify with that also.

Thank you.

A. Thank *you*. Other questions?

Q. My name's Maureen.

A. Hi.

Q. Hi. I've been studying the Course for about a year. I was brought up Catholic as well, yet in working with the Course I feel like I'm undoing all my Catholic "stuff." I'm constantly unraveling and undoing and understanding more about guilt and projection and the ego and all that. And believe me, it's been an eye-opener for me. At first I felt like I was committing a sin when I joined a group studying *A Course in Miracles*. I didn't want anybody to know, any Catholics to know. And so I still feel a little odd about it. Yet I feel very comforted, and very much at peace when I study the Course, and when I participate in groups like this.

A. Oh, I'm so glad to hear that. Thank you for that. Someone else with a question?

Q. Frank, I'd like to hear you respond to the thought that there *is* evil in the world.

A. Well, I'll be talking more about that when I discuss the ego. But the thing I like about the Course is that it puts things in a right perspective as far as cause and effect are concerned. Once you think there's some evil out there in the world, what you're doing is projecting your own self-hate, and your own wish to be cruel, and your own murderous thoughts, out onto a figure called the devil, or Satan, or whatever you want to call it. And that's a cop-out. You're really copping-out when you say, "It's out there." It's not out there. It's in your own distorted, mistaken mind; not *evil* mind, but *mistaken* mind. The title of my first book is *From Guilt to the Gift of Miracles: A Memoir of Mistakes Mended*. Mistakes. So all the evil that I have done in my life— and I've done my share—they were mistakes; mistakes for which I'm *a priori* forgiven. *A priori*, meaning I'm forgiven prior to even making the mistake. Not later. So nothing really happened.

There were times when I treated my wife abysmally. But when I reflect on that, I can see great joy in the thought that I did not hurt her in my abysmal treatment of her. The only way my behavior could hurt her is if she chose to believe she was hurt. Because if I think I hurt her, I have deprived her of the right to decide to be hurt or not. Just think of that. I'm robbing her of the freedom of choice. Do I want to do that?

And the same if anyone thinks they are hurting me. Now I will illustrate that later with a very dramatic story. If anybody thinks they're hurting me, and I believe them, then I've chosen to believe that. I could believe something else. For instance, I could believe what the Course teaches, which is that all that I'm hearing is a desperate, anguished cry for love from the figure who is attacking me viciously; calling me all kinds of names. As I said, I'll illustrate with a story later. (*To another audience member*) Did you have a question or a comment?

Q. Yes, I was thinking about your comment …

A. Oh, good! That's my point—we want to get you to *think*.

Q. Well, I read *Absence of Felicity*—about Helen Schucman's life—and I've been to a number of workshops. I remember one year I was with (*unintelligible*) for a weekend; and he took great offense at my commenting that Helen didn't get it. It seems to me she had fears; towards the end of her life, she developed so many doubts. There's no doubt that intellectually she certainly understood the Course.

But I think that because she was so helpful to so many people, and she did listen to Jesus, well, to that extent, she did get it in her heart.

A. I think it was off and on. Like most of us. Yes? We get it and then we lose it. There's no judgment. Thank you very much.

This is cool! I like all these questions. (*To another audience member*) Go ahead.

Q. I have a question about love. I've always known that I'm here to love. And I've been reading the Course, and listening to what you're saying. And what I'm wondering is that, if love is all there is—and there's a part of me that believes that—why is it that it's, as you said, such a slow process of realization?

A. Because you're stubborn and arrogant. (*Laughter*) How about *that* for an answer? And I'm speaking for me and for everybody else in the room, and for everybody else out there! We are so egotistically preoccupied with "I want what I want, and I want to run my life! To hell with love!" Basically.

Q. Does it *have* to be a slow process?

A. I think so. But some people can do it fast; and I have a story to illustrate that, which I will tell later, about a quick turn-around in an amazingly short time. (*To another audience member*) I believe you have something to say.

Q. Part of the slowness of it is the care taken, in loving, of bringing *everyone* to God.

A. Yes, yes. Excluding no one.

Q. It can't be done fast because of fear; the prevalence of fear. So it's done slowly. It has to be loving.

A. Right. And another way of saying the same thing is that the problem is you think you are your body. And once you think you are your body, you are in a state of panic—when your physical, or your psychological, needs aren't met. So I'm pleading with you: Give up that idea. (*To another audience member*) Go ahead.

Q. I really enjoy the Course, and I'm getting a lot out of it. But something I'm having trouble with is the idea that nothing exists. Not even a beautiful sunset. I have to say I don't get that at all. I acknowledge that it's necessary to learn love and to learn we're not a body. I would admit that we're in this body, but we're not it. We're a spirit going through this lifetime dealing with the physical world—this dualistic world.

A. I agree, the world is dualistic in its ideas. Yes. And I understand that you have a body. Don't deny that. But see that you are not it. You are that spirit.

Q. Okay, so you can do that and still say the body is sitting here in the chair, right?

A. You *think* you are that body sitting in the chair. You're in heaven now *dreaming* that you are a body sitting in that chair. That's the Course's metaphysics. You're in heaven now, dreaming a nightmare of sitting in a chair or standing with, perhaps, an aching back from having shoveled too much snow! (*Laughter*)

Q. Right, and you're a spirit—with a sore back! (*More laughter*)

A. You are solely a spirit of compassion. But you use the body to shine that light of the spirit to your brothers, as I read a little earlier. It's a vehicle.

Q. Thank you.

A. You're welcome. Any other questions?

Q. I'm reacting to your use of the word "nightmare." I mean, there are a lot of things that are truly uncomfortable. And I have this picture of nightmares as being truly horrible, but they're not necessarily so. They're just upsetting, perhaps a little frightening; but there's a lot of different things that I think would come under the heading of "nightmare."

A. Thank you very much. There can be a lifetime that is a nightmare; as well as the nightmares we dream at night. The Course's view is that there is a sleeping dream; and there is a waking dream. You've heard the nursery rhyme "Row, row, row your boat/Life is but a dream?" Life really *is* a dream. You think it's real. Yes, you think it's real. Yet you will wake up one day and say, "My God, I put so much emphasis and effort into all of that, and it was only a dream!" And that's when you cross over. When you cross over, you'll get a different view about what this life here is all about. We do not know what anything means here. That's another lesson in the Course Workbook: *You do not know what anything means.* Well, who wants to hear that? Nobody. So we skip over that one very fast.

Another question?

Q. This concerns a question that I asked Ken Wapnick.[2] I can't remember exactly where in the Course it says that if we are truly peaceful, everyone around us will feel peaceful as well. So I asked Ken about Jesus, just before he was crucified. Basically what Ken told me is that everyone around Jesus at that point *did* experience the peace—at least momentarily—and then the old ego fear kicked in and we saw what happened after.

A. Yes, yes. You can count on the ego fear kicking in. That's for sure. Thank you.

I believe you there in the back have a question—You know I'm beginning to wonder whether I'm going to get to the rest of my talk! (*Laughter*) But it's wonderful!

Q. Frank, I loved your story about the woman and her daughter who wanted to hug you and just be close to your spirit. That's a lovely story. Recently I read an article that told a true story about a gentleman on a train. And a woman was sitting near him with a small baby.

---

2 Kenneth Wapnick is head of the Foundation for *A Course in Miracles*. Ken worked directly with the scribe of the Course, Helen Schucman, in editing the Course into its final book form. He is, in this author's view, the most authentic teacher of the Course ideas alive today.

Well, the baby started screaming inconsolably and just wouldn't stop. And the people around her became increasingly uncomfortable, to the point where several of them got up and moved to another car. Well, this gentleman just sat there quietly sending beautiful messages of peace to the baby. And gradually the baby calmed down and grew quiet and finally fell asleep.

Well, when the woman got to her stop, she came over to the gentleman and she said, "I just want to say thank you." The gentleman was shocked, and asked, "Why?" And she said, "For whatever it is you were doing to make my baby feel better."

A. Wonderful! She got the message. By the way, I have a similar story that also takes place on a train, which I'll tell you later.

I'm going to end this question period now, because I want to make sure I have enough time to cover the things I wanted to talk about today. So here we go!

3

THE METAPHYSICS OF THE COURSE

The metaphysics of the Course are crucial. And in this regard, I'm grateful to Ken Wapnick, because he is, I believe, the cardinal teacher of the Course alive today. He keeps reminding me, "Frank, don't deviate from the metaphysics of the Course."

It starts with a myth to explain why we are so selfish, self-centered, craving for love, yearning for power; yet capable of compassion and gentleness (as in that story about the gentleman on the train one of our audience members told; or, as in Lesson 108 from the Course Workbook, where you practice extending gentleness or kindness or forgiveness to whomever you know is in need of it; and it *is* conveyed).

Heaven, according to the Course, is seen as an undifferentiated state of Oneness. That statement is impossible for us to comprehend, because we have a dualistic brain; so we cannot possibly understand what that statement means. "Oneness joined as One" is another way the Course puts it. Yet that is what we are. We are not individuals. We are one spirit of Love; in forms that we believe make us separate individuals—which is a mistaken idea.

The myth goes that we were in that state of Oneness—Heaven being a state of mind—and a "tiny, mad idea" crept in that suggested to us that we could be a separate individual, a "me" that could say, "Hello,

I'm over here! Recognize me!" But Love does not acknowledge this "me" that shouts, "Hello, I'm over here!" In other words, God can count only to One. And when I say, "I'm over here, and you're over there," that's more than One. So again, it's the identification with separation that brings us our pain.

And we somehow believed, in that moment when the "tiny, mad idea" crept in, that we had destroyed the Oneness. An impossible and arrogant idea of course, which *didn't happen*, but we decided in that mythical moment to hide from God; to flee from heaven by making a world where there are differences, where power reigns, where Love is diminished, and where our specialness is something we all want to believe in—the specialness of being uniquely me. Sometimes our specialness takes the form of believing we are inferior to others; sometimes superior. And you can pick which one you want. It doesn't matter which you pick—they're both in error.

Having believed we have destroyed this Oneness, we are guilty. And we flee to a world where we think we will find love, love apart from God. We think we will find in the world love and understanding, and that our needs will be met. Of course what we actually find is disappointment. The world disappoints. Our yearning for completion—because we think we are lacking something—results in an anguished pain and suffering (and by the way, the Course in this respect is akin to Buddhism, which sees the world as replete with pain and suffering—the Holy Fact of Suffering, as the Buddha expressed it).

There's also the idea that the figures in our life that are special—our wives, our husbands, our children, our parents, our lovers, if we have affairs—are there, specially, to give us the feeling of being whole and beloved. They are, in the words of the Course, "shabby substitutes for the Truth;" the Truth being in our own minds—that is to say, we have right there in our minds the whole, sure, shining light of Compassion. And the figure "out there" that we are relying upon is a shabby substitute because those figures—inevitably—fail us. They may have a pain in their belly and at that point no love to give; or they may have dementia as my wife had the last five years of her life—and increasingly she wasn't present to me. Or we have death, and there's loss. Or we have divorce, and there's loss. The world is unreliable. But we in our stubborn insanity keep relying upon the world, to our detriment. That's the Course's idea.

Also, before we come here, we decide upon a "script" for our lives. As Ken Wapnick puts it, we make a DVD in which I've included on my DVD that all of you will be here at this talk, and all of you have put on your DVDs that I will be here: and at this moment all our DVDs are meeting at this single point in time.

Some of the scenes we have chosen for our DVDs have been very painful. So then we ask, "Why do we make painful choices?" The answer is that you probably chose them because you thought you needed to be punished for your evil ways, for your guilt. The Course says that what we make, out of guilt, the Holy Spirit uses as a lesson, or a classroom, to heal our minds. That's the attitude, the Course's view of how to heal—to take what we made in our misery, out of guilt, to the forgiveness, to the Oneness, available to us in our minds.

That means we can change our DVD script. I write in one of my books[3] about a life-long belief I had that I would meet my death by falling off a sail boat in open water; that the boat's motor would be running and the boat would sail off leaving me alone to drown. How about that for a miserable end? And I held this strange belief for forty years! That shows how much guilt I had. I mean, I really had it up to here.

Well, I did fall off my boat one day, in the middle of Long Island Sound. And the motor was running. And I just managed to grab the boat's gunnel and hold on. And it was November. I had on a lot of clothes and they were soaked through with freezing sea water. And I was over 70 years old at the time. Well, I couldn't pull myself back up in that boat. And I thought, "God, am I gonna make it back into that boat?" Because I knew I couldn't last longer than thirty minutes in that freezing water. I thought to myself, "This is really the end."

---

3   *From Guilt to the Gift of Miracles: A Memoir of Mistakes Mended.*

Well, do you know what got me back in that boat? I heard a voice say to me, "You got more to do, Frank. Get the hell back in that boat!"[4] And you know what? I got back in the boat. My son told me at the time that there was no way he would have been able to climb up into that boat, and he's twenty-five years younger than I. He said, "Dad, I don't know how you did that." Well, I don't know either. But I know it's because I asked for help. I'd prayed to the Beloved One, "Please help me. I've got more to do here." And I'm glad I did. So you see, you *can* change your DVD, the script of your life.

Our purpose here is to be a healer, and to reflect the healing of that Light we have to our brothers. That brings happiness. Here are a few of the principal Course ideas, which I'll state as aphorisms:

Guilt is the cause of all our misery, and it hides love.

Fear is endemic because we have identified with our bodies, and therefore perceive ourselves as being at risk in the world.

Fear hides love as well. We actually fear love. (And I'll give you, in a little while, several illustrations of how we fear love.)

Sickness is a choice. And all pain is also a choice.

The world of separation is a projection of our minds. It is not real. Only love is real.

⌘　⌘　⌘

So do you have any questions or comments on the metaphysics of the Course?

Q. Frank—the subject of guilt which you just referred to is a difficult one for people in pursuit of the Course to grasp and to apply to their own lives. The metaphysics of the Course talk about guilt or—ultimately—"killing off God," as Ken Wapnick puts it; killing off God by choosing the ego, and in effect destroying our Maker in our own minds; and then going off on our own, driving our own boat as captain of our own lives, and so forth. And yet fearing our Maker; projecting

---

4　In a way, the voice I heard was reminding me of a phrase from Lesson 155 of the Course Workbook: "Forget not He has placed His hand in yours, and given you your brothers in His trust that you are worthy of His trust in you." (*W-13:4*)

onto God what the ego would view it as—a betrayal of our Creator which is demanding His retribution. That's the ego thought.

But it's hard for people to make that real in their own lives, if that is an appropriate interpretation of guilt from the Course. And yet guilt is the centerpiece of the ego, of the destructiveness and pain of the ego. Can you help us understand that a little better?

A. Yes, I think I can. That idea that we're guilty because we destroyed Love, I believe lies at the very bottom of our minds, and is totally unconscious. I don't mess with that when I'm working with my patients or with my groups, because it's so abstract. I like to deal more with thoughts that cross our minds that are vicious and judgmental. When those thoughts occur to us, we instantly experience guilt, because we're not loving. We're either in a compassionate, loving state; or we're in a hateful, judgmental, attacking state, which is a state that *always* creates the guilt.

I like Lesson 93 from the Course Workbook, which starts with the wonderful statement, "Light, joy and peace abide in me." Yet the sentence that immediately follows is: "But you think you are the home of evil, darkness and sin." You think that if anyone could see who you really are, "they would recoil from you as if from a poisonous snake."

You think that if you could see who you *really* are, you would rush to take your life by your own hand; for, as the Course says, "living on after seeing this would be impossible." Now I think that is where we really are; but most of us deny that, and say, "I'm really a nice guy." And the reason we deny it is because it's so ugly a thought, we have to repress it. Here Freud comes in handy with his idea of an unconscious mind which is the repository of all ideas we cannot tolerate about ourselves. My view is that I have healed my mind when I've been able to look at how ugly the thoughts are in my head.

One of my earliest experiences in this regard came when I was a kid watching my mother killing flies with a fly swatter. She'd swat a fly and say, "I kill one, and ten others come to the funeral." And I thought, "I'm going to please my mother. I'm going to take care of flies." So I go downstairs to the basement, feeling very virtuous, since this is about pleasing Mother. And I start catching flies. And I would tear their wings off—with great glee. Then I'd put them in a little prison I'd fashioned using a cork and some pins, and I'd watch them desperately trying to get out—again, with great glee; with a joyful feeling—no, it wasn't joy—it was a sadistic pleasure. And then when I got bored with seeing the flies in their prison, I took them out and tossed them into a spider web and watched the spider kill them.

Now when I tell that story, people frown. They're probably thinking, "What a disgusting little fellow!" (*Laughter*) I agree with them! After all, I'm the home of evil, darkness and sin, when seen from the viewpoint of those murderous and sadistic thoughts in my mind. Yet I have learned to look at those thoughts and say, "Yes, those thoughts are there, *but it's not a big deal.*" Because, folks, those thoughts are not me! That was me as a little boy believing I needed to project my self-hate out onto the flies; and mete out to them the kind of awful punishment my guilt told me that *I* deserved.

Later when I was an eighteen-year-old lieutenant in the army, first learning, and then instructing others, in the use of the bayonet, I discovered I still had that sadistic glee. We worked with a dummy made up to look like a Japanese soldier; and the technique was to scream like an animal as you thrust the bayonet into the guts of the dummy, and then twist it. And I discovered that I began to feel happy—no, not happy—"gleeful" is the word; gleeful at the thought of murdering another human being, in this case the hated Japanese enemy. And then one day I said to myself, "My God, Frank, you're a good Christian boy of age eighteen. What are you thinking? Is this Christian?" And the answer was, "No, Frank. Something's wrong with your mind." And then I felt guilty, of course. But later, the Course helped me to free my mind from the guilt.

I think it takes some form of compassion for us to be able to look at the ugliness in our minds. There's a great quote in Chapter 16 of the Course Text that goes:

"Be not afraid to look upon the special hate relationship, for freedom lies in looking at it. It would be impossible to know the meaning of love except for this. For the special love relationship, in which the meaning of

love is hidden, is undertaken solely to offset the hate but not to let it go." (T-16.IV.1:1-3)

All of us want to have a nice, smiley face—called "special love" in the Course—covering up the darkness. We don't want to go there because it's so awful to look at. But the Course's view is that you are forgiven *a priori* for all the dark thoughts.

When I look back at that child I was who could be so cruel, or that young man thrusting the bayonet, I see that it was nothing more than a silly state of mind. I acted with cruelty, yes, but I'm forgiven those unreal thoughts. I remember that only love is real. And that gives me great peace.

Does that answer your question?

Q. Yes, it does.

A. Good! Another question?

Q. There are two things I'd like to speak about.

First, you just discussed recognizing things we've done in our past and acknowledging them; and realizing that you have grown from this, and you've gone away from it. But you have to let those things go. Some people keep them.

A. That's right.

Q. They keep rehashing the past. When the sins are forgiven—or the mistakes—they're thrown into the deepest sea and should never be retrieved. But we punish ourselves, mostly, by bringing them up again.

The other thing I wanted to speak about was the fact of sickness. Now we could say that we've caused the sickness; but the situation I'm facing right now in my own life is that I'm waiting to have a pacemaker put in. This is no imaginary thing, you know. It's going to take place. But whatever I did in the past to get myself to my current state is over. There's nothing I can do but accept what I have now. And not feel guilty about it; and not feel fearful about it. I also had melanoma, and people normally get upset about things like that. But whatever you've been handed, or what comes in life, you accept. You don't give yourself over to guilt or fear, God's in His heaven, and whatever path He leads me on, I will follow.

So that's what I had to say, about guilt, and about sickness. There are things you have to accept, things you have to do. And you have to always know that He's there, and He will protect you. And it doesn't mean He will make me better.

That's all I wanted to say.

A. Thank you. In terms of illness as a choice, I think much illness is chosen before we come here, and put into the script of our DVD. My wife, I believe, had chosen five years of dementia—severe dementia—before she came. It had nothing to do with her guilt at the particular moment in time she developed the dementia.

But the way the Holy Spirit uses that is to help you see that you have another option; and help you to not blame yourself for what you have chosen.

Q. I'm remembering when I was a child, I was in the hospital for 21 days. And I had visitors exactly twice. And you think as a child, "Well, if I was sick, they would love me." My parents were dead at this time, so I'm talking about my siblings. So then you realize this is *their* problem. If they can't reach out to me, it's not my problem.

A. That's right. Good, it's not your problem. No more questions? I'll go on then.

4

THE THREE-PART MIND

Now I'm going to talk about the three-part mind. And I've drawn a little diagram here that might help you visualize what it looks like.

A CASE OF MISTAKEN IDENTITY

GUILT

EGO
- I AM MY BODY
- I AM LACKING
- I WANT POWER
- I NEED, USE, EXPLOIT
- I FEAR LOSS AND DEATH
- I AM CRUEL AND WISH TO KILL
- I AM A SEPARATED, LONELY VICTIM
- I PROJECT MY GUILT AND ATTACK
- I FEAR LOVE YET SEEK IT

CHOICE

SPIRIT
- I AM SPIRIT - NOT A BODY
- " " THE RIGHT MIND
- " " A THOUGHT IN THE MIND OF GOD
- " " SAFE & HEALED & WHOLE
- " " JOINED TO ALL IN LOVE
- " " FORGIVEN & FREE TO FORGIVE ALL
- " " INNOCENT
- I REFLECT THE LOVE OF GOD TO ALL
- MY HOLINESS BLESSES THE WORLD
- THE HOLY SPIRIT IS MY GUIDE
- A STILLNESS OF AN OPEN TRANQUIL MIND

(*Points to diagram*) Now you can see that the three parts are delineated as, first, what the Course calls the Ego, up here; second, the so-called Holy Spirit, down here; and third—here in the middle—the part of the mind that is able to make a choice between the other two.

The reason I've drawn a broken line down the middle of the chart is that the part above the line is the part of the mind that's made up by us. And what we make up is insane. It's our egotism.

The part of the mind below the line comes with our creation, and is divine.

And I chose to title the chart as I did because all the problems we suffer as human beings are caused by a case of mistaken identity. We identify with our body. And once we identify with our body, we are filled with needs. Wapnick calls the body a "need machine."

Now I've listed here in the Ego part of the mind the deluded ideas that we make up:

"*I am my body.*" I identify who I am with my body. That means we identify with death and suffering.

"*I am lacking.*" This is the idea that something is missing in me. How many people here have *not* experienced a feeling that something is missing in you? (*No one in the audience raises his hand*) Right. I appreciate your honesty!

"*I want power.*" I recently worked with a patient who is on "pot" twenty-four hours a day, driving his children in a car under the influence of marijuana, and his wife is worried about that. So I asked him, "What's the purpose in taking marijuana?" (You know, the Course is always urging us to ask of any behavior, "What's the purpose? What's it *for*?") And in a loud voice, my patient answered, "Power!" Well, I knew then that I was dealing with a guy who really wanted power more than he wanted love; more than he wanted to take care of his children, if he was driving them while under the influence of pot.

"*I need to use and exploit the world*"—because I'm lacking something, and because I have a body filled with needs. And I use and exploit especially the special people in my life: my wife, my children, my parents, and my friends.

"*I fear loss and death.*"

"I am cruel and wish to kill." Now I've put that quite bluntly because I believe all of us have that cruelty, as well as a wish to kill. All anger is basically a wish to kill. When I was a kid, we played baseball after school. And a kid named Josie was the only one of us who had a bat and ball. So we needed Josie! Now Josie was Catholic, and there was a Catholic church up the street that rang its bell right at six every night, announcing evening mass. And immediately we'd hear Josie's mother calling for him from two blocks away. And Josie would grab his bat and ball and run off saying, "My ma will kill me! She'll kill me!" Of course, what he meant was that she was angry at him. But we knew— as children—that when there was that tightness of the lip, or the narrowness of the eye, or the loud cry from a parent, that it was our death. Now we didn't really know that intellectually, but unconsciously we knew it, because we were little bodies. And when the big bodies were angry with us, we were at risk. Risk of abandonment, or murder.

"I am a separated, lonely victim" is another idea in this part of the mind.

"I project my guilt and attack"—meaning that I dump my guilt onto others, and attribute my attack thoughts to them. Projection, as the Course puts it, is nothing more than "the outpicturing of an inner condition." That's all we do here: we either project our guilt; or we extend love.

The final one is *"I fear love, yet seek it."* We come here, as I said earlier, wanting to seek love in the world, but basically we fear it. And I will illustrate that later with a couple of stories.

Then there's the so-called second part of the mind—"so-called" because in truth it is the total mind; while it is the ego that is illusory, something we made up, and which consists of all the mistaken thoughts which end up in guilt.

Thoughts in this second, "Spirit" part of the mind include:

"I am spirit—not a body." This means my identification here is not with my body. I, correctly, identify myself as spirit.

This part of the mind is what the Course calls *the Right Mind*—the compassion and love that's in my mind.

"I'm a thought in the mind of God."

"I am safe, healed and whole."

"I am joined to all in love," excluding no one; not Hitler, not Osama bin Laden, not my wife—everyone. (I added my wife because I'm proposing that there just might be the occasional hatred of the wife, or the husband, among those of us here? (*Smiling*) Only occasional, mind you.)

"I'm forgiven and free to forgive all." Again, that's *all* my brothers and sisters, excluding no one.

"I'm innocent." That means innocent *a priori*.

"I reflect the love of God to all" (when I've chosen to heal my mind of the darkness).

"My holiness blesses the world."

"The Holy Spirit is my guide." The last five lessons of the Course Workbook have as their essence: *Be You in charge, Holy Spirit, by my request.* That means I give up my egotism, and my need to run my life.

And finally—as a consequence of our realizing the thoughts in this Right Mind—we experience *"the stillness of an open tranquil mind."* These words come, again, from the last five lessons of the Course Workbook.

By the way, these lines I've drawn emanating from this Spirit part of the mind represent what the Course calls the "Great Rays." The Course says we have a spark of holiness within us, and that the rays of the Light of heaven are continually shining on us and through us, connecting us to all our sisters and brothers, and to our Creator. A prayer I use regularly throughout the day is from Lesson 232, which goes:

"Be in my mind, my Father, when I wake, and shine on me throughout the day today."

And as I say that prayer, I think of the Great Rays shining on me and on all my brothers and sisters, excluding no one.

Now the third part of the mind is what I've designated here as "Choice." It is our ability to choose—to choose either the mistaken thoughts of the Ego, up here; or the right-minded thoughts of Spirit, down here. Ken Wapnick refers to it as the Decision Maker.

Choice is crucial. And I believe it came with Love, because the freedom to choose comes with love. Freedom was a gift to us at the moment of our creation. So we are free to choose, either what we *think* is better for us; or what Love *knows* is better for us. And 99.9 per cent of the time, the Ego is what we choose. That's where we live most of the time. And when—through our freedom of choice—we make a correction, we go to our Right Mind; and then we have the peace.

Now I used a high percentage—99.9—because I think it's vital that you observe how very frequently you are in the ego state of mind. Observing in this way is the process of healing.

The reason I believe we live in the ego most of the time is that we believe we are a body. And therefore we are selfishly preoccupied with me, me, me. At least that's my experience, and the experience of people who come to me in pain.

Are there any questions about the three-part mind?

⌘ ⌘ ⌘

Q. The last ego thought on your diagram—"*I fear love yet seek it*"—I totally relate to that. Can you explain to me why we fear love?

A. Yes, I can. I hope I can make it understandable. On second thought, I'll tell you what I'll do. If you'll stay for the rest of the presentation, I have a story about a patient of mind that will illustrate for you how we fear love. Okay?

Q. Yes.

A. Anyone else have a question?

Q. It's my experience that my motives at any given moment are mixed. When I make a decision, or choice, some of my motives are clearly self-seeking, egotistical. But there are also what I think are more altruistic, loving motives. Isn't it a question of which one of those predominates?

A. That's the world's view, that something can be both true and false at the same time. Or partly true. Or partly false. This belief in ambiguity is the cornerstone of the world's thinking. We want our cake and eat it too.

Sorry, but the Course's view is that you're either in one mind or the other. It's either the ego, or the Holy Spirit. It's either true or false. Real or unreal. Never both.

Is that the question you were asking?

Q. Yes.

A. Then that's my answer!

Someone else have a question?

Q. Do you have a definition of the Great Rays, according to the Course?

A. The Great Rays are a symbol of the fact that you have never separated from the love of God; that there is an overarching Unity to existence. As I say, there is this unity. You are in heaven, with the love of God shining on you, *dreaming* that you are here in the Illusion. So you need what is an equally illusory idea, a symbol, of great rays "coming down from heaven," connecting you to your Creator, and to your brothers. We think we're here, living our special individual lives. We need symbols to help us.

But in truth there are no Great Rays. There's only the Oneness joined as One. Yet given our dualistic, split minds, we *need* an image such as the Great Rays, *pointing* us towards the truth.

The Course is kind. It meets us where we are. It uses our insanity, the language of our insanity, as a start, to help us gently go along to where the truth is.

Q. I'm a little confused about the Decision Maker. Spirit is beyond the body. It is eternal. Ego is—I think of the ego as embedded in the body—but it seems to be something beyond the body as well—

A. It's a thought in the mind that's insane.

Q. Yes. And the mind is not the brain. It's beyond the brain.

A. Yes.

Q. So the Decision Maker is beyond our body. I tend to think of the "Choice" as a conscious choice that we make—through the Decision Maker, from moment to moment—whether we want to be in the Ego or with the Holy Spirit. But when Wapnick talks about the Decision Maker, he's talking about something different from what I understood it to be—which was as more of a brain-choice. I decide from moment to moment whether I choose the Holy Spirit, or the ego.

A. That's the Decision Maker operating.

Q. Okay.

A. The use of the word "you" in the Course refers to the Decision Maker; the One Who Chooses. And the Decision Maker appeared at the same time as the "tiny, mad idea," which was the thought we could somehow be separate from God (this is all according to the Course mythology, which means none of this actually happened). The Decision Maker appeared as a corrective to the now-split mind; which means that at that point we had a choice; whether to listen to the tiny, mad idea, or not. That choice is the freedom that Love has given us. Without that choice, we'd be doomed—doomed to live in the hell the ego has made.

Another question?

Q. I remember one time having an argument with my husband. And I went to my bedroom all exasperated, saying to myself, "Oh, why can't he do the right thing?" And then I heard an inner voice say, "Well, what about you?" And I answered, "I *do* do the right thing." And the voice said, "Then you should know better not to argue and get upset."

A. Well, I'd look more closely at these "shoulds" and "oughts." Whenever I hear those words from patients in my office, I say, "Wait a minute. I don't want to hear 'shoulds' and 'oughts' in this office because that's part of your insanity. Let's take a look instead at why you would believe in the kind of self-imprisonment that you make with these 'shoulds' and 'oughts.'" Those words are guilt-based.

Anyone else have a question?

Q. When you speak about the phrase in the Course, *Be You in charge, Holy Spirit, by my request*—Is the sense of being led what you are talking about?

A. Being led?

Q. Yes, being led.

A. Absolutely. It's a matter of giving up needing to be in control of your life. Which takes courage, because all of us are control freaks.

We're all walking around with a psychic gadget that we can click and—what do you call those gadgets that control your TV set?

Q. Remote control.

A. Yes, remote control! We want remote control over the world, right?

Q. Right.

A. It's giving that up and saying, "Tell me what to do, Lord, and I'll do it." It takes courage. But I invite you to go there, because that is where peace is. You don't know what anything means, so when you make a choice on your own without asking for His guidance, you can't know that the choice is a loving one for you, because the ramifications of any choice you make are far too complex for you to know. If you can admit that, that's humility. And one of the consequences of the spiritual state is the humbleness of admitting that you don't know what anything means.

For example, I had a wife who, in the last five years of her life, needed care. I changed her diapers when she was incontinent. I put her to bed. I fed her. I could have complained and seen that as a burden—I could have seen myself as a victim. Yet I chose not to. I chose to ask instead, "How can I learn how to be a caretaker?" You see, I'd been raised with the belief that only women could be caretakers. When, as a child, I skinned my knee, I didn't run to my dad—I ran to my mom. But with my wife Martha, I learned how to be a caretaker. That was real cool. That was a privilege. Think about that.

You have a question?

Q. Because *A Course in Miracles* uses theological terms, I think it's difficult for people who identify as agnostic or atheist to receive the Course as much as they would or could if those theological terms weren't there. Could you talk about that?

A. Yes, I agree with that. I think it is true. The Course really came as a corrective to the Christian religion. My wife, for instance, had problems with the unapologetically patriarchal language of the Course: terms like "God the Father," "Son of God," or the way the Course refers to our fellow humans as "brothers," never as "sisters." So she went through the Course writing in the word "Daughter," instead of the word "Son;"

"God the Mother," rather than "God the Father," right? So my attitude is, "Fine, change the names!" And you don't have to believe in God for the Course to be helpful to you. What you do have to acknowledge is that you have a spirit of Love in your mind that is eternal, which never dies, and which can't be hurt by anything that happens to you in the world. But you don't have to believe in God. *I* do, because I believe that the Source of my being is that Love that is beyond my personality and my body; the Love which is all-encompassing. And I call it "God." But you can call it anything you want: Moses, Buddha, Mohammed, Spirit of Love, whatever word or figure you are comfortable with. It doesn't matter what the words are. It matters what your state of mind is. It needn't be an obstacle to receiving the Course if you are an atheist. I have a couple of children who are atheists. Imagine that! And I say, "Go ahead, be atheists." But they are basically fine people who are capable of loving. So it's no big deal. Does that answer your question?

Q. It wasn't my question. (*Laughter*)

A. Excuse me?

Q. No, it was somebody else's question.

A. Oh, I see. Whose question was it?

Q. (*Another audience member*) It was mine, actually.

A. Oh, were just too shy to ask it?

Q. No, I just didn't quite know how to state it.

A. Well, did she say it well for you?

Q. Yes, she did.

A. Have you thanked her for saying it so well? (*Laughter*)

Q. Well yes, I have.

A. That's a form of love, by the way—to thank her.

Any other questions? No? Then let's continue.

5
THE PROBLEM OF THE BODY

As I mentioned earlier about the body—the problem is we came into the world as a helpless baby, needing someone to care whether we lived or died. So we learned to depend upon a figure out there in what the Course calls "the living dream of the world;" a figure in the world like a parent or parent substitute who would care whether we lived or died. None of us here would be alive now had we not had someone, in our infancy, who cared for us. We would be dead.

Many babies don't make it because no one wants them to be here. Death can come in two forms when you're a baby: it can come by being abandoned, to the winter storms, where you freeze and starve; or it can come through murder. Speaking of murder, a patient of mine, a woman, was regressed by a hypnotist to age six months; where she experienced her mother trying to strangle her. Now I don't know for sure whether that happened or not, but it certainly does describe the woman's memory of—or attitude towards—her mom; which was vicious hatred of her.

It's the infant's terror of death that causes the child—the infant—to build a persona of defenses to ward off danger. We've all built our own defenses depending on what seemed to work when we were children. The ego is born in childhood, and we as adults continue to respond with that persona we formed in childhood ("persona," of course, is from the Greek word meaning mask, referring to the masks the ancient Greek actors would use to portray different characters in their religious plays). We each have a mask of our personality that is not us. And the persona is a defense mechanism that's set up to protect us from the danger of our bodily helplessness. Yet the personality is not you, the body isn't you. The spirit is you.

In that state of helplessness, then, we have a need for others to take care of us. I'd like to read you the lyrics of a Beatles song to illustrate this point (My kids were into the Beatles. I didn't get into them— I was too old when they came along!). The song is called "Got to Get You into My Life:"

I was alone and I took a ride,
I didn't know what I would find there,
Another road where maybe I could see another kind of mind there.
And suddenly I see you;
Did I tell you I need you
Every single day of my life?
You didn't run, you didn't lie.
You knew I wanted just to hold you.
Had you gone, you knew in time we'd meet again,
For I had told you you were meant to be near me.
And I want you to hear me say we'll be together every day.
Got to get you into my life.

Now that's a description of a special need, for a special person. And most of the songs, in my childhood, as well as in yours, are about this need. I remember particularly a song popular when I was a kid called "You Are My Sunshine, My Only Sunshine." "*You make me happy when skies are gray.*" And if you're not there, I cry. So it's need, need, need. And we call it love. That's the insanity of it all.

There's always the idea of a special one, since we all feel we are lacking. In one of my books,[5] I talk about that marvelous section in Plato's *Symposium* in which Aristophanes, the great Greek

---

5 *Healing Our Special Relationships.*

comedian, tries to answer the question, "Why are we all running around so desperately seeking love?" Aristophanes explains that there was a time—an ancient, mythological time—when human beings were actually two beings joined as one, as a single creature—a creature with four arms, four legs and one enormous head with a face on each side so you could sit around happily chatting with your other half. And these double-humans were of three types: the so-called Children of the Sun, or two male souls; Children of the Moon, who were two females; and Earth Children, a male and a female. And because human beings weren't wasting all their time searching for love, they were immensely powerful; so powerful, in fact, that Zeus became frightened because he felt his power was being challenged. Again, there's the need for power. It's the universal worldly idea.

So Zeus said, "I know how to solve the problem. I'll throw my thunderbolts and slice all these humans in two; and then I'll scatter the fragments over the face of the earth. And these half-humans will then spend their pitiful little lives trying to reconnect with their other halves!"

So, Aristophanes concludes, that's why everyone is searching so desperately for someone else to complete him. If you're a man looking for another man, that means you were, originally, in primeval times, a Child of the Sun; if you're a woman hankering for another woman, you were a Child of the Moon. And you were an Earth Child if you are looking for someone of the opposite sex. So humans are all running around trying to find each other. And sometimes, usually, in fact, they get all mixed up!

Now I think that's a lovely description of the egotism of our special needs, and how we want someone to complete us. Somehow I'm not complete without you. And if you listen to the popular songs— the so-called love songs, which are really *need* songs—you will hear that theme.

⌘　⌘　⌘

Then there's the idea of our helplessness—and the resulting need for power. My wife knew that. And she wrote a poem that describes the two of us together in a room—both of us with the insane need to be right at the other's expense:

What was it we fought about that day?
　So trivial.
　So trivial there's no way I can pull it from
　　the dark depository of memory.

How could it have seemed so important, so right?
　No. It wasn't right.
　　　　I was right.
Ah, yes. That was what was so important about it.
　He was wrong.
　　　Dead wrong.
　　　　　And I was right.

Why couldn't he see that?
　It was so obvious
　Anybody could see it.
Why was he so stubborn?
Why couldn't he just say
　　　You're right. I didn't understand.
　　　　　And maybe add
　　　　　　　　I'm sorry.

Yes. That would be nice.
　I'm sorry would help a lot.

But no. He hangs on to his foolish notions.

Finally I walk away
　Too exhausted to keep up this pounding explanation
　　of my correctness.

Too weary,
   No fight left.

Then the disappointment sets in.
   No. More than that.
     Emptiness.
       Vast cavernous emptiness.

I'm all alone over here on the other side of the room
   In outer space
     Orbiting some unknown planet.
      Lost.
It's so cold out here I can't even see him over there
   no more than the carpet's width away.

There's such a disruption in that space between us.

   A civil war.
   Guerillas ready to drop from the trees
     To shoot when my back is turned.
I hate it when this transparent colorless war breaks out.

How do I get back?
   How do I cross the minefields?

Silence
   keep still
     wait
       keep breathing
         steady now.

Then, shining meteoric flashing in my brain.
   "Would you rather be right or be happy?"[6]

---

6 "Do you prefer that you be right or happy?" (*T-29.VII.1:9*)

That's it. That sorts it out.

Can I give up being right?
No, will I give up being right.
   Well, reluctantly.
      I mean I was right.
Oh come on. What difference does it make?

Then. It's not just having to be right.
   It's having him admit I'm right.

This is really ridiculous.
   He can think whatever he pleases.
   What difference does it make?

Except that I'm making myself miserable over it.

OK. I'm ready now.
                  I can let go.
                     I'm letting go.

   One
      two
         three

It's gone.

Whew!

(*Applause*) I made a lot of mistakes in my life, but marrying Martha was not one of them! It was the best thing I ever did. She taught me what love is about. Of course, in that incident she writes about in her poem, I was doing the same thing on the other side of the room—the other side of the rug, rather.

Q. Did Martha write other poetry too?

A. Yes, she did. But this is one of her most powerful. I'm very lucky. She's still with me, by the way. Everyday. I get a tingling around the face and lips, which a psychic has told me is a kiss. I like that idea. Then I say, "Thank you, Martha, for being here." But then I remember—there is no Martha. There's only the spirit of Love.

So it's power we're talking about. You just heard about the power of being right. Men, on the other hand, tend to want the power of money. I cut an article out of the *New York Times* that illustrates this. How many of you get the *New York Times*? (*Several in the audience raise their hands*) Do you ever read the Style section in the Sunday Times? Well, this is an article from that section, dated January 9. It's an article about love, so-called. It's really about need. It's about a woman, unmarried, in her 40s, and a member of the Mormon church. She feels "left over," like she hasn't got a man. This is what she writes:

I felt like I was left over. I was just never sure what my problem was until one man let me know.

After overhearing a friend and me comparing our weekend horror-date stories, he walked over to me and asked, "You know what your problem is?"

No, I did not know what my problem was. And I was dying to find out.

"Your problem," he said, "is you don't need a man."

"I thought that was a good thing, to be able to care for myself."

He asked if I had a job. Yes. A car? Yes. A house? Yes. Clothes? Of course. Food? Obviously. "That's your problem," he said.

"Excuse me??"

"Men in this church are raised to be providers," he said. "We are the breadwinners, the stewards of the household. If you have all the things we're supposed to provide, we have nothing to give you."

"How about love?" I asked. "What of intimacy, and partnership, and making a run at the world together?"

"Nope," he said. "Men are providers."

Now there are a lot of men who have that inkling, and are probably raised to believe that men are supposed to be the providers. It's a depreciating view of women. I have a couple of patients who are married to men who are evangelical Christians, men who believe there is a hierarchy: first, God; then the man; then the wife, and then the children. In that order of power. The man has the power over the woman, and they both have the power over the children. I think that's an evidence of more insanity, because it's not a matter of equality.

The idea of exploitation is also a part of the dark side of our mind. We use and exploit others. I have three groups of *A Course in Miracles* students, and I asked each group, "How many women in this group married for money?" And do you know what happened? Every hand went up! I said, "What do you think about that? You must hate the men." "Oh, no, no," they protested. "We don't hate our men." "You've got to hate the man," I said, "if you married him for money, and are dependent upon him for that, and believe that you don't have the power in that form. You've given your power over to the man. You've *got* to hate him!"

Well, they hadn't thought about that. Fortunately, they are beginning to think about that.

And how about the ways the Wall Street bankers exploit? Do you remember the phrase often repeated over this last decade, "Greed is good?" That is the idea that I believe led to the financial bubble, which has landed us in the current economic crisis. Greed is good? Greed isn't good! It's a use and an exploitation of others. And when you think about this country, you see clearly that the gap between rich and poor is increasing. I visited Egypt in 2009, I saw policemen at the temples putting their hands out to me—the rich American—begging. *Policemen* begging. And I thought, "Something's seriously wrong with this culture." It had to blow up. Well, our country's in the same kind of danger now—the corruption, and the vast disparity between the rich and the poor. And it's caused by greed. Greed is not good. It is hurtful to everyone. Especially hurtful to the one who's greedy, because guilt always follows.

Then there's the fear of death, which comes from believing you are a body that needs care. Not too long ago, at the various town meetings in this country where Obamacare was being discussed, you would have these men standing up and shouting, "Don't take away my health care!" Which means "I want what I want for me!" Yet what's implied, unspoken, in that statement is, "To hell with the poor." That's greed, yes; but also a fear of death: "I want to save my body. I don't want to die."

When I was aged six, my family had just moved from Illinois to Pennsylvania. My father had lost his job, his house and his career in the Depression, and we had moved in with in-laws near Wilkes-Barre. Now my mom decided to take a few days off to visit an aunt of hers in Manhattan, and she left me in the care of her sister, a good woman who was perfectly capable of looking after a six-year-old like me. Well, I wanted no part of it. I threw a tantrum. Now I have no actual recollection of the tantrum—it's too ugly to remember, how I was so determined to manipulate and exploit my mother in order to get what I thought I needed. No, I was told it later by my aunt and my mother, or I wouldn't now know this story.

Anyway, I threw a tantrum as soon as my mother walked out the door, and I continued screaming and crying—steadily—for a good twenty-four hours before my aunt, in desperation, called my mother in New York and said, "You've got to come home. This kid is inconsolable." My mom came right home, of course. I manipulated my mom to be there with me because I had the illusion that I needed a mom to save me, and I couldn't take anybody else. I was basically an exploiting, manipulating kid. I didn't know it at the time, and I'm forgiven. I just thought I was a body, a body that needed a mom and no one else but mom to take care of me. In fact, a child would be dead if he didn't get proper care. So all manipulation is caused by fear. All exploitation is caused by fear. All greed is caused by fear.

It's an interesting fact that Khalid Sheikh Mohammed, who has admitted to planning the 9/11 attack that destroyed the Twin Towers in New York, and which damaged the Pentagon—with at least 3000 dead—had attended Chowan College in North Carolina, a school advertised abroad by Baptist missionaries. According to the September 13, 2010 issue of the *New Yorker*, Mohammed and his fellow Arab students, in the Muslim tradition, would leave their shoes outside the doors of their dormitory rooms. This made them an irresistible target for the other (Christian) students in the dormitory, who would often steal their shoes and throw them into an adjacent lake. At other times, these students would lean garbage cans filled with water against the doors of the Arab students, knock on the door and run away; and when the young Arab men answered the doors, the garbage can would tip over and flood water into the room. The article continues:

He (Mohammed) told investigators that he had little contact with Americans in college, but he found them to be debauched and racist.

Mohammed returned home to Kuwait, where his old high school teacher, Sheikh Ahmed Dabous, sought him out and found him radically changed: "When he goes there to America, he sees Americans don't like Arabs and Islam. He's a normal boy before—kind, generous, always smiling. After he came back, he's a different man. He's very sad. He doesn't speak. He just sits there."

Now something happened to that boy when he was humiliated by his fellow students at that Baptist college, something that would cause so much hate in him that he would plan the awful 9/11 terrorist attack. Humiliation. Humiliation that led to murder.

Think about a Muslim father who feels humiliated if his unmarried daughter loses her virginity—humiliated to the point where he will have his daughter killed, by his son, if not by himself. This is not uncommon in the Muslim world. And such murder is caused by the murderer feeling he has been debased and humiliated, just as in the case of the planner of 9/11.

It's important, then, to look carefully at the special hate we have; because it's only by looking that we can take that hate to forgiveness, and heal it. And then we don't have to act out that murderous thought.

All attack is a projection. A good example is Elliot Spitzer, the former governor of New York. He was a great one to hate the prostitutes and the pimps, and to launch a statewide crusade against them. Yet all he was doing was projecting his own guilt out onto the prostitutes, because, at the very same time, in secret, he, a married man, was compulsively sleeping with prostitutes.

When I was a kid, there was a preacher in a church nearby us, who could always be counted upon to preach against fornication. And it turns out that this preacher, who was married, was sleeping with the organist all the time he was condemning fornication from the pulpit. He was projecting his guilt out onto others. That's what we do. That's what we all do.

We dump the guilt in order to claim our innocence. It's an attempt to feel special, and separate, and be able to be here in this sinful world, but not be the one who's bad. We love victimhood. All of us. It's important to see that it is an ego state which can also be taken to forgiveness.

I once had a patient, a man, who was into pornography. He was deeply guilty about it. And he would come to his sessions with me and complain about his wife, how she would flirt at parties with other men. He felt she was being untrue, unfaithful to him when she showed attention to other men. Well, I helped him, gently, to see that he was projecting his self-hate for his preoccupation with pornography out onto his wife, saying, "Look what she's doing to me." It's an attempt to gain a false state of innocence. If you can see that, it's very helpful in getting free of it.

There's also a fear of love. The fear is that if we really enter into love, and give ourselves totally over to love, we are basically going to disappear. It's as if we will vanish, losing all of what we thought we have been. It's too frightening for us. That's what the metaphysics of the Course teaches to explain why we are so frightened of love. We want to claim a separated state, because we think it protects us; protects us, above all, from what we see as annihilation. If I were to allow myself to disappear into the light of Love—which is God—where would I be?

Other ego defenses we use are placation, taking the role of peacemakers; or we become detached and withdrawn; we become rebellious, assuming in the family the role of the "black sheep;" we become self-sacrificing, martyrs. We are deceitful because, if we truly believe we are "the home of evil, darkness and sin," and we say to someone else, a spouse perhaps, "I love you; I'm devoted to you;" well, something in us knows that we are lying. We have to deny that dark part of our mind first. We feel fraudulent. The Course says, "Go there and look at it. But look with kind and gentle eyes; not the eyes of judgment."

Basically all this ego garbage I've been talking about comes from a half-baked brain, the undeveloped brain of childhood, when our ego and all its insane misconceptions are crystallized. And from a half-baked brain come half-baked ideas. A fully baked brain is one that recognizes that the ego ideas are false, and which embraces the ideas of the Holy Spirit. That's a fully baked brain. And it tastes—or rather, feels—so good!

Any questions about the dark side?

Q. It's pretty dark!

A. You bet it is. But thank God that the holy Love of God in your mind is far more powerful than all the darkness.

Q. Which of your books is your wife's poem in?

A. It's in *From Guilt to the Gift of Miracles*, and I recommend you get it. I'll read you what I wrote as an introduction to that poem. I think you'll find it interesting:

"Several days after I finished this book I was awakened in the middle of the night with the thought: 'Add Martha's poem as an appendix.'

That sounded right, for Martha had been my best teacher, as the reader knows by now. Her poem deals with the pain that arose when she and I chose to listen to the egotism that led to our not infrequent conflicts. Best of all, it describes the peace that would come when we chose to make the correction and listen instead to the Love that forgives within our minds.

A few years ago I read this poem in Beijing to a group of Chinese and American family therapists, who responded with much gratitude. I hope the same will be true for you, dear reader."

Q. Thank you.

A. You're welcome. Other questions?

Q. You've mentioned Freud a couple of times.

A. I did indeed.

Q. And you just have used the term the "dark side," which is a Jungian concept.

A. You bet it's a Jungian concept. Put Jung and Freud together and you'd have a great combination.

Q. Do you want to speak to your use of the "dark side," in its Jungian sense?

A. I'm not a Jungian. But Jung did understand the dark side. No question about that. Yet I can't really speak authoritatively about Jung. Are there any Jungians here who can? No? I'm sorry then, but I'll have to fail you in that regard. Anybody else?

Q. Yes Frank, thank you for sharing that poem. It's beautiful. I just wanted to share a poem by Rumi that I recently read. It goes:

There is a field beyond right and wrong: I'll meet you there.

A. Yes, I know that poem well. I love it! Thank you very much for reminding me of that. There's another quote by Rumi that I have on the wall in my office. It goes:

Listen O drop: Give yourself up, and gain the Ocean.

And that's about the surrendering of your individual "drop-ness," to the largeness of the ocean of Love. Rumi had it! My wife and I were in Turkey several years ago and we attended a lecture by a professor of philosophy and religion at Istanbul University. Rumi happens to be buried in Turkey. And this professor read several poems by Rumi, in the original Persian. Now at that time, I was totally unfamiliar with the work of Rumi, but when this professor finished reading these poems, in a language I don't speak, I turned to Martha and said, "I think I just heard forgiveness." And sure enough, the professor begins interpreting what he's just read, in English, and it's all about forgiveness. Now I don't know why I got that, but I got it. It may have been the way the man was reading, in his manner—he was extending that idea of forgiveness. But Rumi understood forgiveness. The true forgiveness, which does not come from judgment. Anybody else here know Rumi? (*Practically all raise their hands*) Yeah, there it is. If you don't know him, get acquainted. You will love him.

Q. Frank, would you quote that Rumi poem again? The one on the wall of your office?

A. *Listen O drop: Give yourself up, and gain the Ocean*. It's another way of putting what Jesus says at the end of His Workbook: *Be You in charge. For I would follow You,/Certain that Your direction gives me peace*.[7] The same thing. Different form. Anybody else with a question? No one? Let's move on then.

---

7   *ACIM, Workbook, Lesson 361-365*.

6

HEALING

I want to remind you that our purpose here in the world, according to the Course, is to heal our minds so that we can reflect the light of compassion and forgiveness to all our brothers and sisters. *All* our brothers and sisters, leaving none out. Leave one out, and you haven't forgiven anybody, because we're all one. Again we come back to the holy concept *Oneness joined as One,* which is so abstract that our dualistic minds have a hard time holding on to that, or even understanding it.

Start with the idea that you are not your body. You have a body, and its purpose is to reflect the Love, but you are not it. You are the spirit of Love. But to really connect with this spirit of Love which is what you are, you must be willing to say, "I hope I have been wrong in all my ideas." That's what my wife was able to do in the poem I read to you. She chose in that moment to give up her need to be right. She said instead, "I hope I've been wrong, by holding on to my hatred. What I truly want is the happiness." And she quotes the Course in her poem when she says, "Would you rather be right or happy?"

Pain can be a value in healing. It's a place to start. And so welcome pain. People come to me all time complaining about their spouse. I'm a marriage and family therapist, so I encounter a lot of situations where the husband is blaming the wife, and the wife is blaming the husband. They are pointing the finger of blame at each other, and I invariably ask them to point instead at themselves. Now that's a metaphor that clarifies exactly where the problem lies. It does *not* lie in the other person. It lies in your own mind.

I had a woman who came to me as a patient some years ago. She came to me because she had been, for over seven years, in excruciating pain. Any number of doctors, any number of different therapeutic modalities she'd tried, had all failed to help her, and she was coming to me, in desperation, because somebody had recommended the Course to her in general, and me in particular.

She was 52 years old and had never married, though she had dated a lot of men in her life, and had come very close to marrying a couple of times. In both cases, she had backed out literally days before the wedding, suddenly overwhelmed emotionally by the prospect of being married, and unable to go through with it.

The pain was in her teeth and, as I said, was excruciating, and constant. She could pinpoint the exact instant the pain began. She had been dating a man, and he had kissed her, a very passionate so-called "French" kiss, in which his tongue had entered her mouth. At that very moment, she experienced blinding pain in her teeth, a pain that, from then on, was with her day and night.

When she told me the story of how her pain had started, I asked her to write it down, because I might want to use it sometime in a book, if that was okay with her. She said, "All right." But then she said, "But Frank, I'm afraid of writing it, because I don't think I write very well." Well, I'm going to read you what she wrote, and you tell me whether or not you think she was temporarily insane when she said she doesn't write very well!

"I suffer with teeth pain, and the multitude of experts I have seen have failed to discover why. Searching for ways to deal with pain, I was told about A Course in Miracles, *and given Frank's name.*

At our very first meeting, Frank asked me why I was choosing to live in pain. Well, no one in their right mind would choose to live with this pain I have. But the idea of choice meant I had control.

So I started reading and applying the daily Course lessons, with both hope and doubt."

(What this woman did was that, each day, she would write down the topic of the lesson on a piece of paper, and then she would look at it frequently during the day, as a reminder. Now, if you've noticed—those of you who've worked with the Course—once you read something in the Course, you forget it. I can read a passage in that Course, and a minute later, I say to myself, "What the hell did I just read?" When I read the *New York Times*, I can tell you what I read. And that's because the ego does not want to hear the truth! It wants you mindless.)

"On the seventy-eighth day, the lesson title was: 'Let miracles replace all grievances.' As the Course suggests, I closed my eyes, and trusted that the names of the people I hold grievances with would come to me. Well, in a very short time, I saw an image of John, a man with whom I had spent seven years in a romantic relationship, from ages 21 to 28. I am now 52 years of age.

The second image was of my mother. For all of you who have had a mother, I need not say more." (Laughter)

(You recall when I told you about another patient of mine who remembered being strangled by her mother at age six months? True or not, that's a common picture of motherhood!)

"Next as instructed by the Course, I looked upon them with all their faults, and—in their human form—how they hurt me. Oh, this was easy.

When asked to look upon them in a different way, and see our savior shining in the light of true forgiveness, the challenge started. Every time I tried to break through the barrier of hatred, I learned I did not want to let go of the hate. I could not forgive their ways of silent manipulation and cruel judgment. If I were to let go of the hatred, they would not see how much they hurt me. They would be let of the hook, so to speak.

Knowing in my mind that this was a crucial point of self-awareness and healing, I stayed with the hatred, to see how it served me."

(P.S. Great move.)

"Much to my surprise, I saw myself standing in silent manipulation and judgment. Recognizing my part in this, I tried to bring forgiveness to John, mom, and myself.

Still no luck. The block of hatred was still there. So I took a deep breath, and stayed with the block."

(P.S. Good choice.)

"The longer I stayed with it, the more apparent it became that, if I forgave them, I would be left alone. The blocked hatred, manipulation and judgment were my way of keeping a connection with them.

Frustrated, and stuck with the idea that I would be connected to them through negativity forever, I asked for help."

(P.S. Good move.)

"Soon I heard Frank's voice say to me that we are all born with our own DVD, our own pre-determined path. In that moment, I was able to see John and my mother as actors in my movie."

(You recall my daughter Laura, and the voice that spoke to her on a street corner in Manhattan, saying, "Look around you, everything you see is a movie you have made up?")

"Their role was to bring me to this place where I am standing. In this new view, I was able to see how I had stayed disconnected from the light in others, through silent manipulation, and cruel judgment.

The next image was that my mother and John were turning into automobiles. They then transported me through the darkness, and the muck. I was brought into a light where I was able to let go of the hate, and felt a pure joy and love for them as they drove away.

I have never experienced such a sense of freedom, and physical looseness. My head, neck and shoulder were relaxed, releasing the pain."

I can add that when I saw her after she had written this and brought it to my office, she said, "The pain is 80% reduced." And it had been an intense and unrelenting pain for seven and a half years. That's the power of forgiveness. That's the power of the Course. That's the power of doing the Workbook. Do it! It heals.

Notice too that this woman was disciplined, she wanted to look within, and she wanted to ask for help. Those are the ingredients. That's all you need, the willingness to say, "I don't want the pain."

There is a lovely epilogue to this woman's story. She writes:

"The next day I received a call from my sister Sarah. She is a very healthy woman who takes good care of herself. But for the third time this season, she woke up with the flu. So I asked her, 'Why are you choosing to be sick?'"

How about that for the passing on of a healing idea? Now what's interesting about the last part of her story is that this woman's sister was someone who was not at all close to her, and who normally called her only if she wanted something from her. Now notice, I don't believe it was a coincidence that this sister, who lived many miles away, who very rarely called, happened to call the day following this woman's miracle of forgiveness. That's what love does—it extends beyond time and space. As the Course puts it, "Love flows across the world with quiet joy."

And it's important to be diligent in watching the flight back to darkness. I have another patient, a young woman, who just had a baby. I'm telling this particular story as evidence of the ego's retaliation to our choice for happiness. This woman was unmarried, the pregnancy was unexpected, but she decided to have the baby anyway. So she had the baby, decided not to marry the man, but she wanted to keep the baby. So I asked her, "You seem quite happy with this baby. Yet you had, at the time you got pregnant, three choices. Why did you choose to keep the baby?" "Oh, that was easy," she said. "I just asked what would make me happy."

And she was obviously very happy, nursing this baby, and feeling that love that a woman can feel as she nurses. So then I asked her, "Do you ever have a thought—when you're especially happy—that something's going to happen that's going to foul it all up, and that the happiness will end?" And she said, "Oh, yeah. Right now especially." Well, I thought that meant the baby, so I said, "What's the form of the thought that crosses your mind, now that you're so happy with the baby?" And she answers, "You see, I have a house with radiant heating in the floor, so the floor is poured concrete. And sometimes when I pick up the baby and carry it across the room, the thought occasionally crosses my mind that I will drop the baby, and his head will hit the concrete, and that that will be the end of the baby." Now that, folks, is the ego's retaliation, particularly when we are experiencing happiness.

Another example of the ego "flight from love" is expressed in a dream one of my patients had, in April of 2009. This is a man whose father was a general officer in the Air Force during the Vietnam War; the top general, at one point, responsible for the bombing campaign in Vietnam. And as this boy was growing up, his father would move the family from base to base, so the kid was the new kid in the school every year or two. So he was always the odd man out, feeling lonely. He was also gay, and knew it early. His mother was alcoholic, and his father was preoccupied with being a general, so this boy was very much at sixes and nines.

So he longed for some figure that would be always with him in his loneliness. Well, he chose Jesus. A useful image. In the Course, Jesus says, "If it will help you, take my hand; and I assure you it will not be in vain." So that is what this man did early in his life. And this man has been having dreams in recent years, dreams about Jesus and him. And this is one of his dreams:

"I am on the shore with Jesus. The sea is a gently swirling body of clear white light. He says, 'Let's try it this way: Put your toe into the water first. If that is all right for you, put more and more of your body into the water.'

I do so. It feels good, the water warm, life-giving, reassuring. I am in over my waist. I decide to 'take the plunge.' Suddenly I am immersed in the gently swirling sea of Light. I look at my body. It has disappeared into the bright transparent light. Yet I do not feel lessened in any way. In fact, now I can feel myself as the whole ocean, intimately in touch with every part of it. But where is Jesus? I no longer see Him. Yet I feel Him there— all around me, flowing around and through me like water. The contact is intimate and relaxed and joyful like nothing I've known on earth. A total communion.

Suddenly in the distance, through the sea of white light, I hear a sound that I recognize as the voice of God. It is flowing closer, and I know that soon it will surround and interpenetrate me as Jesus has. In the first instant I am pleased, delighted. The next instant frightened. I know if I join with God, there will be no turning back. 'I' will be lost forever. It is too much for me, and I wake up."

Now this dream was followed immediately by a vision.

"I lie awake for a while thinking of the dream. I am looking at the ceiling, and the near objects in my room. Suddenly I 'punch through' the familiar objects and find myself looking at what is 'behind' them. It is a gently rotating, silent vortex, tunnel-like, deep purple and indigo in color, in texture cloud-like. It emits an unearthly calm, peace, safety. It is pulling me gently in. Suddenly I am afraid again. I pull back, back through the veil, and the familiar objects in my room become visible again, and I am afraid."

Now the very next day following this dream and vision, the man became sick. He writes about that as well:

"In a strange way, I believe that my illness followed as a result of the dream and waking vision I had Wednesday night. I think I felt the need to pull back into my body through illness, into the pain and discomfort and weakness which somehow focus us more completely on the body and its needs. Remember that both in the dream and in the vision I grew frightened of entering wholly into the light, into the joining, into the total loss of self (though I know, intellectually, that what is gained in doing so is the True Self, the Christ). Yet I feel I have truly seen that Joining. I know what it looks like. And I know that it WILL come."

How about that for a dream and vision? And what a wonderful illustration of the flight from the love we actually fear. We fear it because we think we will disappear. And in this man's case, the figure of Jesus, which is so beloved to him as a comforter and a companion, would disappear along with him.

So the final point I want to make about healing is this: the Course posits the notion that the Son of God cannot be hurt. And I have an illustration of that.

I have three groups of A Course in Miracles students that I use as therapy groups. And I have a woman in one of the groups who is very volatile in her emotion. And I have another woman, in the same group, who's very tightly controlled—you hardly know what is going on behind this very controlled exterior, behind these well-knit defenses.

And these two women go at each other. They hate each other. So I usually try to use their hatred so that I can talk about projection. Well, one night, something very different and unexpected happened.

Now unbeknownst to me, the tightly-controlled woman had just that day decided to divorce her husband, whom she'd married, in part, to provide a green card for him. I did know, however, that her mother had died just a few months before, and that this woman had chosen to separate, in anger, from her father and her brother. Her brother had been abusive of her as a child, and her father had stood by while she was being abused. So I knew those things, but I did not know about this woman's divorce plans.

So on this particular night I walk into the group promptly at the start of the hour. And I've hardly sat down, when the volatile woman starts criticizing the woman I've just described as having decided to get a divorce. Whereupon this woman drops her usual tight control and dissolves into tears, screaming, "This is an unfair, unsafe place. I'm being attacked. I cannot stay in this group any longer. I'm going to leave and not come back. I may come back in six months, but I'm not sure."

Well, I was surprised and shocked, and the other group members were surprised and shocked. We went on with the group, but I couldn't figure out why this blow-up had happened. So I thought to myself, "Well, that's the end of that, she'll not be back." This woman had been very vocal and forceful in stating that she was through with the group.

Well, I was wrong. The group was on a Tuesday. The following Monday afternoon, I got a call from this woman. She said, "Do you have an hour available today—I'd like to talk to you." I said, "Sure, I happen to have one hour open." So she traveled quite a distance to come to my office.

Usually when a patient walks in my office, I give them a hug. I think hugs are healing. I was taught in my training not to touch patients, of course—which is crazy. Anyway, as I reached out to embrace this woman, she pushes me away, with glaring eyes.

She takes off her coat, throws it on the couch, and sits down. Then for the next forty minutes, she gives me hell: "You're just like my goddam father. He stood by while my brother abused me, and you stood by and didn't stop it while I was being attacked in the group. And you're not a thoughtful therapist, and I can't possibly continue to be in that group which is an unsafe place for me…" And she went on and on and on.

I decided to do what the Course recommends, which is to see beyond appearances. The first four paragraphs of Lesson 109 refer to appearances—looking beyond appearances to the holy light in the person who is viciously, murderously, hatefully attacking. This woman could have killed me. I could feel it, feel the intensity of her hatred.

So I saw the light in her beyond the hate. I did not defend. I didn't say anything. I just looked with that state of mind of non-judgment.

As I said, she gave me hell for forty minutes. So we have five minutes left in the hour (I call it an hour—it's actually forty-five minutes; I cheat a little bit!). I said to her, "I learned later from members of the group that you had decided to get a divorce that very day of our meeting. I didn't know about that. I knew about your mom's death, and about your severing relations with your father and your brother, but I didn't know that you had chosen to part from your husband as well. And I hope you will forgive me if I was insensitive to what you were going through, and not picking up what was going on in your mind when I walked in the room last Tuesday night."

Well, I saw no visible response in her. She got up, and she threw a check on the table. I said, "No, this hour is on me." I don't usually do that. I like getting paid, so I don't really know why I did that… No, I *do* know. I heard a voice guiding me to do it. So I followed that guidance. But that's very uncharacteristic of me.

So I went to hug her, and she stood there rigidly while I hugged her. I got nothing back. Then she went out. I thought, "Well that's the end of that."

Wrong. The next night I walk into my Tuesday group, and she's sitting there. I said to her, "Well, that was a fast turn-around! Would you stand up?" So she stood up, and I hugged her. And this time I got a very big hug back.

I said, "My God, would you tell me, please, what turned your head around?"

She said, "It happened in your office. Yesterday."

I said, "What happened?" Because I didn't think anything happened. Wrong. It shows how ignorant I am.

She said, "Three things happened. I gave you hell for forty minutes, and you did not judge me (In the words of the Course, "love listens, waits and *judges not*.") The second thing that happened was that—at the end of the hour—you said to me what my father would never have said. You said, 'I hope you will forgive me for being insensitive to your state of mind.' I saw at that moment that you are not like him."

I said, "What was the third thing that happened?"

"Well," she said, "that was the most important thing. About two-thirds of the way through my harangue of hate, your face began to shine and glow with a brilliant white light. It finally shone so brightly, I could not distinguish the features of your face."

I said to her, "You had a miracle!" Which indeed she had. I didn't even know it had happened. But I believe that she was extending her light and love (which, by the way, I was at that moment working consciously to be aware of in her, beyond the appearance of hate and attack)—she was extending, as I say, her light back out onto me—and then saw that light coming back. And that's what we do. The healing occurred when I established a non-judgmental environment, and her love responded to that, in that instant. And that was the *holy instant* that the Course talks about. That's our purpose in healing our own minds—that we might offer that healing to our brothers and sisters and experience the joy of that sharing.

When she told me what she told me, I felt such joy, that I had been a part of that experience to help her heal her mind of her hate. I mean, what could be happier than that? And that's something every single one of us can do, if we put our minds to healing the so-called 'dark side,' which is an insane complex of illusory, false ideas—all mistakes—and instead choose to listen to the Holy Spirit only.

Are there any questions?

⌘　⌘　⌘

Q. This is a thought that we've brought up in our group, but when I was hearing you speak of the man with the dream of Jesus, followed by the waking dream—

A. Yes, the vision.

Q. –and both times pulling back from a complete immersion; well, it seems to me that the fear of love is very tightly linked, in my view, and in the context of the language you use, with the fear of death. I've often thought that to become completely in my right mind, to totally give up the illusion of my body, is congruent with the state of death.

A. Well, it's the death of the ego.

Q. Yes, the death of the ego. I think that's what the man was pulling back from in his dream.

A. That's right.

Q. And I was feeling his fear, and thinking to myself , were I to have followed that dream completely to the place it was leading—total union with God—well, they would have found me eternally asleep.

A. Yes, you might decide to leave your body, permanently, at that moment, and be caught up wholly in the arms of God. Or you may decide to keep the relationship with your body, so you can share what you saw, and your understanding of the truth, with your sisters and brothers, here in the illusion. But one thing is certain. You *will* return to total awareness of God as your Creator. You *will* get there! The outcome is assured.

By the way, several months following the dream and waking vision I just read you, the same man had another waking vision, again with Jesus as his companion in the vision. He's had several visions and dreams with this scenario, and they seem to be progressive, each leading successively closer to an experience of total union with God, what the Course refers to as "returning home."

"I am in the low wooden structure on the beautiful sandy beach. Jesus is just outside the door. He has the familiar features, yet this time there is a light emanating from his face and upper body.

I pass through the door to meet him. As I do so, my features become his—and the same light is emanating from my face and upper body.

I am face to face with him. I am looking into my own face, the face of Christ.

Then I take one final step, into him, and the two of us merge into a single figure—the single Christ.

Instantly there is an explosion of light. The light in me-him-us explodes outward to illuminate the entire earth and sea and sky around us; then further outward, illuminating the planets and the sun—which become alive with the most gorgeous and electric colors you have ever seen; then further and instantaneously outward, to encompass the galaxies, the entire universe—whose immense and diverse body is taken in, surveyed and comprehended, in a single glance—a single thought. The colors and shapes—suffused with a tangible, humming sense of beingness—is the most beautiful ever imagined.

Then the galaxies, the worlds in all the myriad of shapes and motions disappear into one immense white light, which suffuses all space and time. They disappear into it. And I and Jesus, joined in the single Christ figure, disappear into it. There is only now the undifferentiated white light, from which emanates a single, cardinal musical tone—indescribably warm and low and reassuring—containing all octaves, all tones, all voices (including that voice which the instant before I had claimed as my single and distinct voice).

I (the little I) am no more! I the Christ am no more!

There is only the great I AM.

But then in the very next instant, the visual of an all-encompassing white light, the sound of the great tone, the very idea of the I AM— even these, disappear, caught up into an eternity of timeless, spaceless Communion that is beyond all description, beyond all reflection.

It is finished."

Now that's where this man moved in the eighteen months since the first dream/vision I read you. Now I do not doubt that this man—despite having this amazing vision—will once again retreat into the ego. In fact, he's done so. But he knows where he's been. And once you know you've been there—it's like going in the woods and finding this wonderful trail—you might get lost again, but you know you've been there, and you can get there again, even though you may get lost many times.

Another question?

Q. I was just wondering about something. I have a fear of success.

A. Yes, you do. You don't think you deserve it, baby!

Q. Yes, that's what I feel.

A. You do deserve it.

Q. Okay.

A. You deserve it! You deserve not only that, you deserve the happiness that comes with success not mattering.

Q. Thank you.

A. You're welcome. Any other questions?

Q. All the way through your reading of the first dream, I was thinking of the similarities between this man and Helen Schucman, and of course I think one could say, as a bottom line, that her resistance was the same fear.

A. Absolutely the same fear. We're all the same! With the same fears. We're not different from each other. That's the good news!

Q. So the other thing I noticed—I believe in the model of the hologram anyway, as opposed to any linear concept of time and space—I was just wondering if this man is young enough to be the reincarnation of Helen Schucman?

A. Well, I just don't know the answer to that question. I believe, however, this man was in his twenties when Helen died. I do know that this man has a memory of a previous incarnation, in which the Roman Catholic Church hanged him, along with his young lover, for the so-called sin of sodomy. This was in fourteenth century France, and this man was a troubadour in that incarnation. The Church also ordered that all the manuscripts of his music be destroyed. Well, interestingly enough, in his current incarnation, this man is also a musician and a composer.

Another question?

Q. I have been a dancer most of my life. My dad died when I was very young, and I didn't know where I was for about two years—

A. I'll bet.

Q. But then I found dance. And in dance I found—well, I found that feeling that says, "It's wonderful up here!" So I underwent a transformation at that point. And I went into a whole lot of areas to try to find out the answer to the questions "What is dance?" and "What is the body?" I wanted to know how dancing had this power to light up our eyes and raise us up.

Some of my life lessons have been very hard.

A. I'm sure they have been.

Q. One of hardest has been during this last winter. And I turned to *A Course in Miracles*, and it was reading that that got me through this winter—

A. Wonderful.

Q. It helped me let go of stuff. I said to myself, "Well, I can't do anything. So therefore, I *have* to give this up." Yet all along it's been like being on a razor's edge not trying to fall into the guilt thing, or fall into the fear, or fall into the hate thing. And I always have to test it in my mind before I move, because I know that will make all the difference. Yet I know that I have some hard lessons. But I'm convinced this is the right way.

And in those moments when I choose out of the fear, choose out of the hate, I see light in people's eyes.

A. Yes, yes!

Q. It isn't an ego thing. I have to always remember the humility of it. But the light that is there. . .! Sometimes I have this feeling that comes over my body, usually when I'm in a gathering like this one. It's a feeling of loving palms coming out and touching me with love and with care. It happens, but only once in a while.

A. Would you stand up?

Q. Yes.

A. Would you walk over here? Because I want to hug you.

Q. Oh, I'd love that.

A. (*Hugging the questioner*) You're wonderful! I thank you for your story.

Q. Oh, thank you, thank you!

A. You're welcome. It's a great pleasure.

Anybody else have a question before I close? No? Then I'd like to finish up, as a meditation, by reading from the epilogue of the Course Workbook.

7
MEDITATION

These are the words of Jesus. He says to us students of the Course, and to those of us who are not students:

And now I place you in His hands ('His' referring to the Holy Spirit), *to be His faithful follower, with Him as Guide through every difficulty and all pain that you may think is real. Nor will He give you pleasures that will pass away, for He gives only the eternal and the good. Let Him prepare you further. He has earned your trust by speaking daily to you of your Father and your brother and your Self. He will continue. Now you walk with Him, as certain as is He of where you go; as sure as He of how you should proceed; as confident as He is of the goal, and of your safe arrival in the end.*

The end is certain, and the means as well. To this we say "Amen." You will be told exactly what God wills for you each time there is a choice to make. And He will speak for God and for your Self, thus making sure that hell will claim you not, and that each choice you make brings Heaven nearer to your reach. And so we walk with Him from this time on, and turn to Him for guidance and for peace and for sure direction. Joy attends our way. For we go homeward to an open door which God has held unclosed to welcome us.

We trust our ways to Him and say "Amen." In peace we will continue in His way, and trust all things to Him. In confidence we wait His answers, as we ask His Will in everything we do. He loves God's Son as we would love Him. And He teaches us how to behold him through His eyes, and love him as He does. You do not walk alone. God's angels hover near and all about. His Love surrounds you, and of this be sure; that I will never leave you comfortless.

Amen. And thank you all very much.

APPENDIX

*T*he attached material—a letter from one of my patients—
illustrates how a disciplined study of the Workbook lessons in A
Course in Miracles can result in a shift away from our identification with our bodies towards an identification with the creative spirit of
Love. It also shows very clearly the Ego's intense resistance to this holy
process.

August 2011

Dear Frank,

Per your request, I'm writing down the meditations, visions and
dreams I've had over the last few days. Perhaps the story I relate here
will be helpful to others.

As you know, I began doing the daily lessons in the Course
Workbook a few months back. This is the third time I have gone
through this process, the first being when I initially encountered *A
Course in Miracles* back in 1989. This third go-around, I am encounter-
ing the lessons with a depth and an understanding and an imme-
diacy that is new, and which, I believe, is taking me to a new level.

What follows is material garnered from working with three lessons over three days—August 7, 8 and 9. As you know, when I am

meditating over a specific Course lesson, I often write down thoughts as they occur to me, in my notebook, in a form of automatic writing.

⌘　⌘　⌘

Lesson 71: "Only God's plan for salvation will work."

This lesson makes an astonishing request of us. It asks that we speak to God directly, asking Him to reveal His plan for salvation to us. It proposes that we ask Him three specific questions. Following are the questions, and the answers that came to me:

Q. What would You have me do?

A. *Look no longer to idols for your salvation. And be assured that those events, situations and people you have seen standing in the way of your Good—of your Blessing—are as insubstantial as a mist, as a dream.*

Q. Where would You have me go?

A. *Relax into your Center where I am. Hold constantly to the hand of your brother Jesus.*

Q. What would You have me say and to whom?

A. *I would have you* listen—*and speak only when guided by me to do so.*

⌘　⌘　⌘

Lesson 72: "Holding grievances is an attack on God's plan for salvation."

Again we are asked to speak directly to God, in the form of this question:

Q. What is salvation, Father? I do not know. Tell me, that I may understand.

Here is the answer that came to me:

A. *Salvation is looking no longer to your body—nor the bodies of others—for your Good. The image of the body is at the center of your understanding of the world. It is your chief and principal idol. It is looked to as the source of your power, the source of your pleasure, the instrument through which your supposed sins are expiated, and—through its death—the vehicle to launch you into a suppositional world of spirit.*

Those bodies you have judged beautiful are worshipped especially by you—with certain parts of bodies prized and worshipped above others. The equating of sexual pleasure and death in your mind is one of the stranger tenets of this idolatry—which has served you for your theology.

In looking to your body—and the bodies of others—for your salvation, you have been looking to nothing, for the body is nothing. It can feel neither pleasure nor pain. It has no power, no life, no motion, no health nor illness—beyond that which mortal mind endows it with.

See—through realizing the falsity and unreality of the body—that which is true and real. The body is a laughably paltry substitute for my Love—which is infinite Life, Being and Truth. That Love is yours as well as mine.

Open your heart to it. Relax into your Center where I am. You are my beloved Son, in whom I am well pleased.

⌘　⌘　⌘

Lesson 73: "I will there be light. Let me behold the light that reflects God's will and mine."

Meditating on this lesson resulted in an astonishing vision, one that came in answer to my inner wish to behold, as the lesson urged me to, the light that reflects God's will and mine.

I'm on the beach with my brother Jesus, who holds me firmly by the right hand. The sky is dark, and sprinkled with a myriad of silver twinkling stars. The air is cool and still—the water moving gently yet powerfully, a dark undulating mass in which there are a million glints of starlight.

Jesus and I stand there in happy expectancy—though, in me, the feeling alternates with flashes of uncertainty, of fear. Yet with the gentle squeeze of my brother's hand, I am reassured.

Now we hear a gentle hum coming from behind the horizon—a cluster of tones harmonious, and so low in frequency, they are felt more than heard. This hum is growing and—in the next instant—light explodes from the wide horizon upward and fills the entire sky. It is so bright I have to close my eyes. "It is too bright! It hurts my eyes," I say to Jesus.

"Don't worry," he says. "Your eyes will get used to it."

He is right. Gradually I'm able to look. The sky is alive with light—light of every color, and of an unthought-of life and luminosity. The colors and textures of the light suggest forms that move and then dissolve into other patterns—sometimes planets and suns—sometimes shapes that suggest faces, benign and holy faces. So delightful, endlessly fascinating—you feel you can watch forever in total delight, and never get bored or tired.

But now I look at my hands, my arms—they seem to be catching the light, and are beginning to glow with it. My whole body is aglow—I look down and see my pulsing heart in my chest, illuminated with a gorgeous light of shifting colors, accompanied by the most pleasant and luminous tones. I feel my face aglow. How wonderful! The light-colors emanating from my body seem to play with the colors and shapes moving above and around me through the sky—and in the water too, which is a sea of swirling luminous color.

Jesus too is aglow in rainbow light. We have halos! I find I can extend and retract mine at will.

"What is going to happen?" I ask Jesus. "Are we going to lose ourselves in it?"

"No," he answers. "You can trust it. We are finding ourselves. We are seeing what we really are. We are coming home. Fear not your Father. He greets us with arms wide open. We are about to be caught up in the arms of Love."

⌘   ⌘   ⌘

Two nights later, following this astounding vision, I had a big ego attack. That part of my mind no longer pulls any punches, nor pretends that it intends anything other than my death.

I awoke about one in the morning feeling as if a strong (Darth Vader-like) hand had gripped me by the windpipe and was squeezing hard. I had real problems catching my breath. It was particularly hard to exhale. I seriously wondered if I were dying.

Yet though it seemed terrifyingly real, something in my mind knew that what was happening wasn't real. I caught hold of the hand of Jesus and held tight. I knew that if I was patient and waited, then the distressing sense of suffocating would pass.

Within an hour it was gone. And the next day, there was no trace of it.[8]

And that day's Course lesson was this: "The light has come. I have forgiven the world."

Amazing! I am so grateful for this deeper understanding of the "flight from Love." Long, long ago I condemned my body to die a slow and tortuous death, spread out over decades—death by suffocation. This was the "just" punishment that would expiate the guilt I felt.

I'm releasing my body now from the terrible sentence I passed on it. I'm forgiven that sad and mistaken thought of pain and death.

Love,
Chad

---

8 Author's note: The fact that my patient's difficulty in breathing lasted only an hour is a significant departure from his experience of the last fifteen years—years in which bouts of bronchitis and asthma had become more frequent and more serious. Seasonal cases of bronchitis would hang on for weeks, and a life-threatening asthmatic condition that arose four years ago when he was fifty-six lasted almost a year and was diagnosed as chronic. Yet in the last three years, instances of these types of breathing conditions have become less and less frequent, and have since virtually disappeared. My patient takes no drugs other than an occasional Advil, and attributes this improvement in his health to his inner spiritual work—and to a greater understanding of the Course's statement that "sickness is a choice" that is made less and less often as one forgives one's mistaken thoughts, one's *guilt*.

10762316R10053

Made in the USA
Charleston, SC
31 December 2011